Love Will Always Light The Way Home

A collection of poetry about love and relationships.

By

S.G. Schuller

I dedicate this book to my mother, Arlene Schuller, who supported and encouraged my interest in the arts from an early age.

To my children, Marques and Kirsten, let this be an example of how it's never too late to take a chance and follow your dreams.

I would be remiss not to say thank you to the numerous friends who offered advice, provided feedback and helped me through this endeavor:

Jayme W., Lawre H., Tony O., Lacie T., Angela L., Donny, Joey L., Jeff M.,

Gabriela D., Carmen B., Pamela O., Kayla O., Bernarda D., Clarence, Florence R.,

Jeff C., Christina S., Dawn K., Tammy L., Iris H., Johnny G., Cindy C., Bethany B., Sidney B., Ada M-D., Dan I., Sam I.

You all gave me support, encouragement and advice that provided the impetus and energy to see this through to its completion.

Each and every one of you had a small part in making this idea become real.

I couldn't have done it without all of you.

Thank you!

This book is my personal perception and view
on love and relationships.
Some observations are sweet and passion-filled.
Others come from the opposite side,
when love and relationships don't work out.

I hope you enjoy this collection—
through the joy and passion,
the pain and sadness—
and find a connection with some of what you read.

—S. G. Schuller

Table of contents

All Of My Love

The days of innocence are long gone,
I couldn't wait to see your sweet smile.
Times I would see the passion and desire, for
me twinkling in your sky-blue eyes.

Days I would burst through the front door to
lay my eyes on you,
Moments I would wrap strong arms around
your petite body in a tight embrace—
Yearning for your luscious satin soft lips to kiss mine.

Incidents of talking and laughing nonstop for hours,
Nights of romantic, passionate love-making til'
the wee hours of early morning—
Waking up, you cuddled next to me your soft
breath rippling across my skin.

Feels like only yesterday we fell head over
heels, deeply in love.
So many big plans and amazing dreams
for our future together.
Today, I realize you are the only thing that
really matters to me.

No matter what life brings or what happens in this world,
There is literally just one thing I want to do for
the rest of my life—
With everything I have and all that I am,
I only want to give all my love to you.

Today You Are A Man

From the day of your conception
That's where your journey did start
Unpaved road ahead milestones to make
From that very moment you were in my heart

As a young boy you were a joy to behold
Watching you grow and play and run
Lessons in life for you I tried to pass on
We didn't always agree even though you're my son

The teen years were tough and trying
You acted like you didn't need me anymore
But no matter what the problem ever was
My love for you always left an open door

There were times you thought I was the devil
From all your problems gave me all the blame
My love for you has never wavered at all
Even when you looked at me with disdain

One day you met someone you grew to love
You decided she had to stay in your life
In time the relationship grew and blossomed
In September of 2014 became husband and wife

It is now a little over 7 and a half years later
A brand-new chapter in your life has began
No longer just a son, brother or husband
Today my boy you become a father and a man

Lifetime of Love/Love of A Lifetime

I wish you a lifetime of love
With the love of a lifetime

I pray it's someone
That always stirs passion in your soul
Whose touch you eternally crave
Whose kiss you forever hunger for
Whose embrace you desire constantly

An individual you
Open your darkest places
Inside your mind to
Reveal every secret you've buried within
Show the scars you've hidden from the world

A special person
vThat when you see them
Gives you instant butterflies
Makes your heart skip a beat
Just a thought of them
Puts a smile on your face

A unique being
That accepts your flaws
Ignores your imperfections
Whose smile melts your heart every time

Someone
You can be vulnerable around
Be completely emotionally naked with
An individual that will
Fiercely beat back your demons
And summon your angels

I pray they are your—
Partner.
Best friend.
Partner in crime.
Confidant.
Soul mate.
Lover

Could I Love You Any More

Could I love you anymore?
Then at this singular moment in time?
You were an unexpected gift,
I still can't believe you are mine.

Could I love you anymore?
Over seven billion people that I could meet.
From the very moment that I met you,
You completely knocked me off my feet.

Could I love you anymore?
My affection for you grows every single day.
Just when my heart can't expand anymore,
You do something that takes my breath away.

Could I love you anymore?
I look at you, the air around you just glows.
When you look at my eyes, I know you can see,
My love for you radiates shines and shows

Could I love you anymore?
The world stops turning when I'm with you.
When you kiss me, it feels like I can't breathe.
There's nothing for you I wouldn't do

Could I love you anymore?
Is it possible to love someone this way?
You are like a real living dream.
My love will grow even when my hair is gray

Could I love you anymore?
I will love you for our entire lifetime.
You keep my heart totally aflame.
There's nothing that my love can't outshine.

Just A Dream

Perfectly shaped lips
Delicately formed,
Deep crimson colored
Pillowy plump full silky soft

Her shiny, wet pink tongue
Seductively sliding across them

Beguiling me
Tempting me
Beckoning to be kissed

Surrendering to her desire,
I acquiesce to her plaintive request
Leaning towards her, hesitantly,
preparing to taste her tender lips

Just as we were about to touch
Suddenly she vanishes and disappears
Like a ghost, like vaporous apparition
That in a heartbeat became totally invisible

I instantaneously snap wide awake
Fraught with disillusionment and deep despair
In my bed all alone
Realization seeps into my consciousness—
She was just a figment of my imagination.
It was nothing but a vividly real dream

Journey Of Love

Forget your head
Listen to your heart
Love is passion
It is not possession
Follow your feelings
Take a leap of faith.

To make the journey
Fall deeply madly in love
Reward is worth the risk
If you haven't tried
You haven't truly lived

Love of a lifetime
It is not someone you can live with
It is someone you can't live without
A soulmate isn't sacrifice
It's addition not subtraction
Pushes you to reach beyond for more
Open your heart to love.

Tell them your desires
Share your fondest hopes and dreams
See the best in someone
Love returned to you priceless
Lights a fire in your heart
Ignites passion's flame in your mind
Awakens your very soul
You may not be their first love
Be their last love and greatest love of all
That is the journey of love.

I Still Feel You

After all these years,
I still can't shake you.
You're forever a part of me,
I still feel you.

When the summer rain falls against the windows,
I still crave your gentle touch.
Wish I could embrace you lovingly,
I still feel you.

Fall leaves turn into their bright colors.
I hear your laughter ringing in the air.
Its sound is so hauntingly real,
I still feel you.

Snow piles up deeply at Christmas time,
I can taste your kiss like honey on my tongue.
Softness of your ruby red lips,
I still feel you.

Our daughter graduated from high school.
Your voice quietly whispers inside my head,
Telling me how proud you are of her.
I still feel you.

I drive by where our house used to be.
It's been gone for over 16 long years.
Scent of ash and smoke still so vivid and real,
I still feel you.

Life is not the same anymore.
There's a hole in the broken heart inside my chest.
That is where you will always and forever live,
I still feel you.

Promise You Will Love Me

Promise you will love me
From our first day until our very last
In granite stone our love is eternally cast

Promise you will love me
With all my flaws and my mistakes
Love me always no matter what it takes

Promise you will love me
For all the emotional gifts I bring to you
Together there's nothing we can't get through

Promise you will love me
Love me when things are bad or good
Just like I always hoped and thought that you would

Promise you will love me
You are a constant song in my heart
From you I forever never want to be apart

Promise you will love me
Brighter than the sparkling stars in the night sky
In so many passionate ways, I never wonder why

Promise you will love me
With unspoken gentleness and serenity
That flows from your soul effortless and naturally

Promise you will love me
through the rest of time for all eternity
together forever It will be you and me

Promise you will love me
With a love that will forever consume my soul
An undying flame of passion, that is my goal

Promise you will love me....

He Loved Her

He loved her mind; he loved her heart.
He loved her completely from the very start.

He loved her through the good times and through the bad.
He loved her when they were happy, even more when they
were sad.

He loved her strengths, and he loved her flaws.
He loved her unconditionally, he loved her just because.

He loved her when they were young, full of life and energy.
He loved her more with the birth of children 1, 2, and 3.

He loved her deeply as the years continued to roll past.
He loved her, there wouldn't be another, she's his first and
his last.

He loved her very much as the children grew up and moved
away.
He loved her as their wrinkles came and their hair turned
silver, gray.

He loved her so passionately in every single possible way.
He loved her more and more deeply with every passing day.

He loved her in a way that very few ever can or will.
He loved her when her health began to fade and
she became ill.

He loved her when she took her final breath in this life.
He loved her and was blessed for all the years
she was his wife.

He loved her……

Love Will Always Light the Way Home

When you feel completely lost
Enveloped and trapped in total darkness,
With no stars or moon to show the way
Let your heart be your souls guide
Love will always light the way home

There will always be a light left on
The door will never be locked
My arms are always open to embrace you
No matter how long it takes to come back
Love will always light the way home

Doesn't matter what you have done
Nothing to be ashamed or embarrassed of
Forgiveness is given no matter what the cost
Unconditional love is waiting here for you
Love will always light the way home

Leave the struggles of your past behind you
No judgments are served or ever allowed
Acceptance for a new beginning awaits you
Let your heart guide your road of retribution
Love will always light the way home

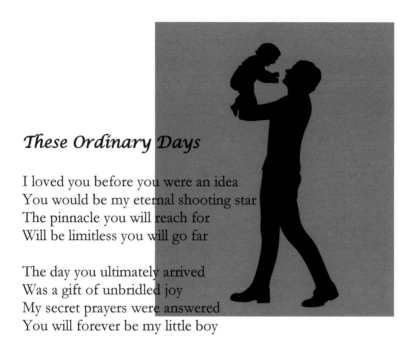

These Ordinary Days

I loved you before you were an idea
You would be my eternal shooting star
The pinnacle you will reach for
Will be limitless you will go far

The day you ultimately arrived
Was a gift of unbridled joy
My secret prayers were answered
You will forever be my little boy

I wish you would stay young
Life doesn't work that way
Maintain innocence as long as you can
Treasure the memories of these ordinary days

To you time moves so slowly
For me the years fly by far to fast
Today will quickly become tomorrow
Leaving those special days in the past

More time with you I wish for
Now you're a young man fully grown
Still, there's so much left to teach you
Soon you will have a son of your own

Dance with your children in the rain
Moments vanish quickly they never stay
Create many keepsake precious memories
Of these ordinary days

Kiss Me

Just kiss me

Kiss me like the first time you kissed me
Kiss me while the sun shines
Kiss me under the moon and stars
Kiss me in the pouring rain
Kiss me like you did behind the barn

Kiss me like you did in the backseat of your car
Kiss me the way you did when we said I do
Kiss me the way you did when we became parents

Kiss me as the flowers bloom in spring
Kiss me with passion of a hot summer day
Kiss me when the leaves change colors in autumn
Kiss me when the snow falls outside in winter

Kiss me by the bonfires on the beach
Kiss me like you miss me
Kiss me so it takes my breath away
Kiss me when times are good
Kiss me when times are bad

Kiss me on days that end in the letter Y
Kiss me while we are still young
Kiss me the same way when we are old
Kiss me when our hair has turned silver
Kiss me because our love is as good as gold

Kiss me good morning every single day
Kiss me goodnight every single night
Kiss me to give me a sweet hello
Kiss me to tell me a sweet goodbye,
Just kiss me...

Forever Fallin' for You

From the first time I saw you from across the crowded room,
I was fallin' for you.
The mischievous twinkle in your emerald, green eyes,
I was fallin' for you.
The innocent, cute way you smiled,
I was fallin' for you.
The first time we slow danced together,
I was fallin' for you.
When I kissed your silky soft red lips,
I was fallin' for you.
The night I asked you to marry me,
I was fallin' for you.
We found out that you were pregnant,
I was fallin' for you.
As our children gradually grew up,
I was fallin' for you.
Every time one of them got married,
I was fallin' for you.
As each grandchild entered this world,
I was fallin' for you.
When wrinkles came and your hair turned gray,
I was fallin' for you.
As we enter the twilight years of our lives,
I was fallin' for you.
On the day the Lord called you home,
I was fallin' for you.
When I see you in heaven someday—
I'll still be fallin' for you.

Love You Forever

The moment I first laid my eyes upon you,
You sent shockwaves straight to my heart
Everything else slowly simply faded away
That's where my love for you did start

I summoned up the courage to approach you
Not having a solitary clue what I would say
Before I spoke you smiled and said hello
Our lifelong romance began that very day

Time has slowly steadily ticked on nonstop
Loving you infinitely more as we grow old
You're my angel gifted to me from heaven
One of a kind after you they broke the mold

I wouldn't trade a single moment for anything,
Of this life's memories we've been through
Each trip around the sun with you by my side
Tells me I was right to trust my heart to you

Each and every chapter of our love story
Is unique in its own individual special way
No one else I would take this journey with
I will love you forever until my very last day.

Love Is Making Me

Subtly, silently love comes to me
Arriving like phantom ghostlike whispers
Floating on the wind
Erotically arousing all my senses
Awakening each one individually, softly
Nudging them bringing life to all of them

Tendrils of amorous passion slowly
Growing, expanding, stirring deep within me
Not with the roaring intense fire of raw
Powerful, carnal lust and desire
But gently subtly, serenely on gossamer
Ethereal breezes

Filling my heart to overflowing
Like a waterfall cascading from my soul
Steadily surging, rhythmically coursing through my veins.
It's essence harmoniously filling,
Enveloping, caressing everything existing within me
When I am not making love,
Love is making me...

Fly My Butterfly Fly

You were just a lonely caterpillar
Awkward withdrawn excruciatingly shy
Encouraged you to be a treasure to behold
Destined for greatness I could not deny

I nurtured you through your metamorphosis
Time transformed you into a beautiful butterfly
Watching you grow was a blessing
To that I will proudly always testify

I selfishly wanted to keep you to myself
That action had no reason I could justify
To release you and share you with the world
Meant one day I would have to say goodbye

Relinquishing you to the world
Is so painful it cuts deeper than a Sai
I know the day is eventually approaching
Fighting back tears trying not to cry

Knowing I must release and set you free
Time to spread your wings and fly
How will I live here without you?
As you soar into that endless sky

It's criminally painful to stand in your way
To your wish I reticently will comply
May you fly with strength and confidence
Soaring to heights they are tough to quantify

Spread your wings go as far as you can go
With your departure flight I'll sing a lullaby
To sooth my soul on the day you fly away
Praying someday you'll return we will reunify

Forever I'm Yours

My heart belongs to you alone
I never knew what love was until I finally found you.
I never thought I could be so deeply
So completely loved by anyone until you.
I've never loved anyone the way I love you.
No one will ever love you the way that I love you.
Loving you gives me dreams for tomorrow.
I want to love you for the rest of your life.
Loving you is the single, greatest gift I have ever been given.
Love is not something you search for; it is elusive because
love will find you.
Loving you gives me courage I didn't know I had.
Having you love me in return gives me strength.
Loving you makes every single day better and worthwhile.
I will always and forever be loving you

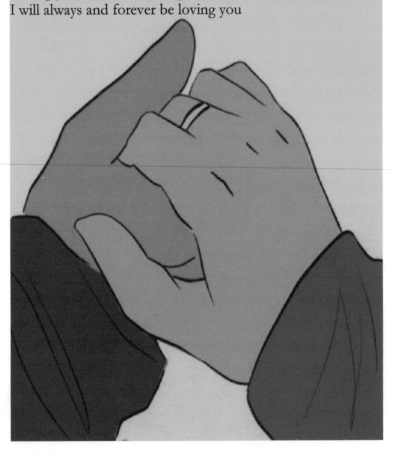

Knowing You're My...

The clouds incrementally float by,
In a gray stormy overcast sky.
Against the window rain gently falls,
Clock slowly ticking time slowly crawls.

In a dark room a restless soul sits alone,
Awaiting an inspirational light to be shown.
To enlighten the path a guide it to its new way,
Where its journey should go from day to day.

With every beginning, there is always an end,
Journey is richer knowing you're my friend.
Memories will be made worth more than gold
With you by my side, through it all truth be told.

Inside My Dreams

In my dreams you come to me
Your touch and kiss I crave to feel
Even though it's only in a dream
I passionately wish that you were real

Your face is like that of an angel
Your gold flexed sapphire blue eyes shine
Your soft, full ruby lips are incredible
I really wish that you were mine

Your beauty is totally spellbinding
You are a dream that lives till the dawn
I cherish every nightly visit with you
but with morning light you are gone

Nightly you visit me in my sleep
We meet on the dreams ethereal plain
In it's mystical, magical fantasy world,
that only exists inside my brain

Will I find someone real like you?
Only time will tell or so it seems
It's you that I will be searching for,
Now you only exist inside my dreams.

I Want To...

I want to wake up tangled up in sheets next to you,
Feel your warm body pressed against mine,
Feel your breath upon my skin.

Slowly run my hands through your silky hair,
Wrap my arms around you hold you close.

Upon waking up, be the first thing you see.
Be your initial thought everyday—
Kiss you good morning each day.

Catch the sunrise with you every morning,
Whisper, "I love you," in your ear.
Be the shoulder you lean on when you're sad.
Wipe away your tears when you cry.
Catch you and be your soft place to fall.

Dance outside in the pouring rain with you.
Tickle you and listen to your musical laugh.
Kiss you each and every single day.
Be the reason you smile unexpectedly.
Be the temptation that makes you late for work.

Sit on a porch swing with your head on my shoulder.
Watch your eyes sparkle when you smile.
Let you know you're loved for all time.
Bring you flowers for no reason at all.

Spend every second with you.
Watch the sunset holding your hand.
Make you, my queen; I'll be your king.
Kiss you goodnight every night,
Dance with you in your dreams.

Create lifetime of irreplaceable memories with you,
Observe your hair turning silver as we age.
Be your lover, partner, soulmate, best friend.
Love you as long as my heart beats
And I have breath in my lungs—
That's what I want with you!

Your Arms Feel Like Home

You are my comfort zone
When we snuggle, I am at peace,
My safe place to fall
Port in the storms of life
Your caress soothes my soul

Refuge from the outside world
Encapsulate me totally within your arms
My sanctuary from daily chaos
Respite escape to serenity
My stillness in the atmosphere's cacophony

Your embrace washes away the days noise
Envelope me tightly in hug
Place of solitude from the world's turmoil
My anchor my saving grace
Your arms feel like home

Romeo And Juliet

I can no longer brush aside and deny
This feeling building deeply inside me
The unique way that you make me feel
I wish you would open your eyes and see

Every time I find myself around you
Within me butterflies erupt taking flight
Words get tied up on my tongue
This torture occurs every day and night

My pounding heart races in my chest
You're more beautiful than any floral bouquet
My palms instantly turn cold and clammy
Your mear appearance takes my breath away

To you I'm your best friend and confidant
You have no idea what I would give for a kiss
I am screaming I'm in love with you inside
I get close, drop hints, you simply dismiss

The bond between us will never be broken
I will always come running whenever you call
To celebrate the highs and also wipe away tears
I wish you could see how I really feel is all

Instantaneously you pierced my soul
That magic moment occurred when we met
As well as capturing my beating heart
I'll forever be your Romeo, you my Juliet

Love Me

Love me just exactly as I am
Love me like you've never loved before
Love me the right way
Love me so I have something to live for

Love me when things are bad
Love me when we're happy
Love me when we feel trapped
Love me when our souls feel free

Love me if we are apart
Love me in different ways
Love me while we are together
Love me for years, not just days

Love me in our early days
Love me in days when we're old
Love me when our hair is colored silver
Love me with your heart as good as gold

Love me because I can make you laugh
Love me even when I make you cry
Love me in snow and in the rain
Love me under the sun or moon in the sky

Love me as your first and last
Love me for our entire lifetime
Love me so it makes all others jealous
Love me with a love extremely sublime

Love me for my mistakes and flaws
Love me for all of my strengths too
Love me for what you truly believe
Love me because I'm the perfect for you

Love me as long as your heart beats in your chest
Love me through all everything we ever do
Love me completely now and forever
Love me the same way that I love you

Love me......

Her Eyes

Looking deep into her eyes,
In that moment he became lost.
He was mesmerized, enraptured—
He had to know her, no matter the cost.

Her eyes were like none he had ever seen,
Felt he was being pulled into her soul
Time seemed to stand completely still,
To stay there forever was his goal.

Their eyes locked on each other,
Everything else seemed to fade away.
They were alone in a private universe,
That's where he wanted to stay.

It felt like it lasted for forever,
But in a second, she vanished so fast.
She disappeared and was gone,
His present and future were now his past.

The woman whose eyes stole his soul—
She's real and exists out there.
Someday he will find her,
Somehow, some way, somewhere

Her Kiss

Plump
Engorged
Silky smooth
Pillowy soft
Scarlett colored.

Lips…
Tastefully succulent
Bright like summer sunshine
Syrupy sweet like honey
Tantalizingly delicious
Delicate like nectar from a rare flower
Passion filled
Hypnotically addictive
Insatiably captivating
Unquenchably delicious
Time altering.

Her kiss.

Your Touch

When your gentle hands tenderly touch me,
And ethereally dance across my skin
Your faint wisp like caress instantaneously
Sends vibrations roaring quickly throughout
The tendrils of my soul

Ripples of electricity course through the cosmic membranes
of my mind
Crashing and cascading through its nebulous universe
Accelerating at lightening quick speed
Faster than a nanosecond of time

Sensations broaden exponentially
Creating increasing rolling waves of pleasure
Which endlessly flow into every crevice
That resides internally within my frame

My synapses greedily and hungrily devour
Any exposure from your amorous embrace
Causing quantum reverberations to echo
Within my innermost cavernous expanse

Your vaporous fingerprints are eternally
Seared adhering to the infinite dimensions of
My spiritual existence that seamlessly
Sinuously bonds with the fabric of my external corium

What is Love

Love is invisible structure,
A shapeless ghost profile,
With no actual proven configuration
Described by poets for centuries
In many forms and appearances
A transient emotion with no singular design

It lives and exists within us all,
They claim it comes from your heart and soul,
But no one truly knows its point of origin

When does love begin?
When does it truly end?
What ignites this passion we named love?

We love various things
family
children
friends
pets
jobs
cars
houses
clothes
places
seasons
holidays
colors
books
movies
music

Is love what defines us
Or do we define what love is?

It's a feeling...

Physically, we can never feel it,
Or witness a silhouette from it

We love hugs
We love how someone kisses us

With so many variables
It will forever remain
A vague aspect
Defined only
By general guidelines and definitions

The question will never honestly be
Resolved with one answer is:

What is Love?

I Love How You Love Me

Your lips feel electric when they touch me
They feel like lightening dancing on my skin
Every time I get close to you air crackles
Excitement begins to build within me
You have me wanting so much more

Your fingers exude a sensuous sensation
They are like a drug that I crave so much
Transporting me to a mystical place
Anticipating the exquisite joy of your touch
Baby hurry and walk through that door

I love how you love me
Our love is honest, pure and real
My promise is to love you like no other
I love how loving you makes me feel
I want the entire world to see
I love how you love me

Words really can't describe the feeling
When you press your sexy body against mine
Our mutual desire is a roaring passions fire
Our sensual dance nightly blows my mind
Can't wait till the moment your dress hits the floor

From across the room when you look at me
With a devious, sultry look burning in you
I instantly know what's in your thoughts
Excitement ignites I know what you want to do
Special love making is what is in store

I love how you love me
Our love is honest, pure and real
My promise is to love you like no other
I love how loving you makes me feel
I want the entire world to see
I love how you love me

You love me in ways I can't believe
It's a love I never expected to receive
Ana ll consuming love that;s out of this world
I can't believe I am your man and you are my girl
v
I love how you love me
Our love is honest, pure and real
My promise is to love you like no other
I love how loving you makes me feel
zI want the entire world to see
I love how you love me

My Thoughts Turn to You

Hard to believe another year has passed
Where has the time gone
My thoughts turn to you

Grass turns green flowers bloom and grow
Birds are singing songs in the trees
My thoughts turn to you

When the rain is falling, thunder rolling
Lightening dancing across the sky
My thoughts turn to you

Leaves change into their autumn colors
Bonfires burning bright against the night
My thoughts turn to you

Snow is piling up outside the door
Bitter icy winds roaring against the windows
My thoughts turn to you

Your clothes are still in the bedroom
Laughter; footsteps ring through the house
My thoughts turn to you

Taillights In The Rain

I know now I lost you long ago
You had gradually started to slip away
I missed the prominent glaring warning signs
Unaware I had been taking you for granted
Overlooking the subtle withdrawal of your love

Only if I had actually opened my deaf ears
I should have listened to what you said
If my blind eyes had really been watching you
It would have been abundantly clear to see
Your love for me evaporated a long time ago

You packed your things in 3 well worn leather suitcases
Every last piece of clothes, every single pair of shoes
Without saying a single solitary word to me
Awkward stone cold silence was thick in the air
Your blue eyes brimming with unshed tears
Lips trembling, quivering fighting for control
Sadness was deeply etched into your face

Standing in the doorway sadly watching you
Resolutely with slumped shoulders
Hands stuffed into my jeans pockets
Mentally I struggled to find the words to say
I was unable to verbally speak physical words
I knew there was no way to make you stay

I stepped aside as you lugged each suitcase downstairs
You swung open the heavy oaken front door
Dragging them one at a time out to your car
Loaded every last one of your possessions
In that rusted, faded blue gray 72 Chevrolet

Lightning crackled across the night sky
Thunder rumbled loudly echoing overhead
Rain began falling in ever increasing numbers
You sat behind the wheel and closed the door
Turned the key and put it in gear
Turned on the headlights and the windshield wipers
Slowly pulling away, heading down the driveway
You reached up adjusting the rearview mirror

If you looked up in the mirror
You couldn't see the tears in my eyes
I didn't want you to see me crying
I watched as you slowly drove away
Leaving me with one final memory
Your taillights driving away in the rain

Her Journey for Love

She thought she would be alone forever.
Around her wounded heart, she built a wall,
But inside of it, the hope of love springs eternal.
For love, she moves forward through each stumble and fall.

Out there somewhere is someone meant for her.
She believes this deeply, heartfelt, and true
With each relationship, she suffered many hurts,
But inside loves eternal hope still shines through.

Through this world, she moves in search of love.
It's her lifelong mission, not just a dream—
One day she'll find what her battered heart yearns for,
Like a movie, she'll be in the perfect scene.

Are there things she regrets along this journeys path?
Yes; but to find love there's losses, risks and gains.
Love's eternal hope is her life's one and only quest.
She will find it come sunshine or rain.

One day her search will finally reach its close.
When she finds love and it breaks her heart's wall down.
All she wants is to be loved for who she is inside,
To be loved like a queen, but without the crown.

Love Me, The Real Me

Love me, the real me
For whom I am deep down inside
I offer you everything that I am
I've no secrets; I've got nothing to hide

Love me, the real me
Accept all of me right from the start
My life is like an open book
I will completely open my heart

Love me, the real me
From this day on, till eternity
I know I will never be perfect
But I will give you the best I can be

Love me, the real me
As the years pass, I will make you smile
Despite my many flaws and mistakes
My love for you will never be in denial

Love me, the real me
As long as my heart will beat in my chest
I will try to make all your dreams come true,
On that I promise to do my best

Love me, the real me
I will make you as happy as can be
Through all of our laughter and tears
That's my promise and guarantee

Love me, the real me
On the day as I get down on one knee
With a ring I will offer you my world
And ask the question, will you marry me

Someone To Love

The sun slowly creeps up over the horizon
The sky in its crimson, lemon, and amber haze
It rises between the white wispy clouds
Its beauty still captives his gaze

Another day is gradually dawning
It's another beginning, a brand-new start
What events will unfold in front of him
To possibly ease the ache inside his heart

He is still completely emotionally numb
His heart still hurts inside his chest
She had been his entire world
He had given her, his very best

The day she told him that it was over
She didn't love him at all anymore
His entire world instantly imploded
His knees buckled, he almost hit the floor

He felt his heart explode and shatter
His mouth opened, but not a word came out
He was stunned, frozen where he stood
He gave a silent scream, yell and shout

The tears started cascading down his face
So many poured out it felt like a waterfall
Inside him there was carnage and chaos
She destroyed his world like a wrecking ball

She left him standing there that morning
Took her suitcases and slowly drove away
That moment happened twelve months ago
To him it still felt like it was yesterday

He makes it through the mental fog of everyday,
But he has no idea of the how or why
Inside he is still very raw and hurting
As he stands and watches the morning sky

Another day was just slowly starting up
He gazes at the awakening sky high up above
He still needs more time to emotionally mend and heal
Before he can once again find someone new to love

The Little Things

Sensuous smile on her ruby red lips
Seductive curve of her salacious sexy hips
Wisp of her perfume hangs in the air
Copper colored ringlets of her hair
A few things of her I adore

She laughs it's the sound of her giggle
When she walks it's her sultry sassy wiggle
Radiant glow of her chestnut-colored eyes
Her tear-stained cheeks when she cries
Those things make me love her more

She runs to me at the end of the day
Wraps me in a hug that takes my breath away
Snuggling in bed with her head on my chest
Whispers I love you and you are the best
Those things make my heart soar

She laughs even when I tell jokes that are bad
Her sassy little pout when she is acting mad
Free spirited she will dance to any song
Embarrassed face if she did something wrong
Little things I love down to her core

She tries to sing and it's always off key
Only person she wants to be with is me
That tingly feeling wither hand in mine
Lets me know truer love I will never find
I will love her for infinity plus one second more

The Day I Met You

I can't explain the way I am feeling inside
I can't believe you love someone like me
How did I ever get so very lucky?

What have I ever done to deserve this gift?
That destiny has rewarded me with you

There are days I think this can't be real
That this is nothing but a never-ending dream
If that's true, I hope and pray it never ends
I wake up every morning, praying you are still,
Beside me.

When you came into my life I was completely,
Lost with no purpose,
Now I have direction, meaning and a plan
I am truly the most blessed man to be with you

The sensations that run through my body
When I'm with your words can't describe
I have never felt so alive except for when I am with you
I feel like a thousand butterflies come to life
Inside me when you are near

Your caress sends shivers clear through me to my very soul
When you kiss me, it still takes my breath away?
The day I met you is when my life finally began
With you everything falls into place and makes sense

The Kiss

The dance was over.
Last reverberations of the ending chords from
Closing song echoed throughout the gym
Resonance of the final notes escaping from the sound system
speakers
Time reluctantly finally arrived to escort his date home

Pale full moon shimmered up above in charcoal colored sky
Stars glimmered and twinkled brightly against the blackness
of the atmosphere
Night air had a crisp, cool clean sensation a gentle breeze
lazily blowing

He walked her home holding her hand
In complete silence without a solitary word being uttered
between them

As they traipsed down the avenue under the dull yellow glow
from the intermittent streetlamps

Fireflies sporadically flickered with their greenish-yellow glow
randomly here and there,
In the air amongst the trees and bushes as they passed them
by.

Only sounds that existed was the orchestra of crickets
chirping that serenaded them
Accompanying their rhythmic footsteps echoing
Off the concrete sidewalk as they strolled casually along

They walked up the path to the front door of her parents'
house
In unison they turned toward each other
Looking each other in the face and smiling at the exact same
moment

He held both of her hands gently and gazed deeply at her
heart shaped face,
Her cute upturned button nose
And lightly dusted rose colored freckled dimpled cheeks
Then finally into her large gleaming emerald, green eyes
Kissed with burnished flecks of gold intertwined in them

He gradually leaned in to kiss her
She closed her eyes breathless with anticipation
She could sense his presence as he drew near her
Around them the air pulsed and crackled
With an intense energy and excitement in it

He drew closer to her full, pillowy, silky soft crimson lips
he could feel her breath
Escape between her lips In slow, soft, ragged gasps
Her lips trembled and quivered with excitement and
anticipation

Faint wisps of her perfume wafted undulating into his nose
Sending her tantalizing fragrance instantaneously to his brain
Her essence intoxicated him;

Her perfume had an allure
With a heady light ethereal aroma

Their lips touched instantly something inside erupted and
exploded
Like a dam bursting wide open came alive within her
Feelings she had never felt before experienced
Rampantly accelerated through her body
Like a tidal wave exponentially gathering inertia

Kaleidoscope of a multitude of dazzling colors danced
Like fireworks decorating the inner surface of her closed eyes
And flit through every recess and crevice
In the hemispheres of her mind

Her breath caught and seized in her tightening chest,
Time seemed to freeze the stillness was almost palpable
Her body vibrated and trembled
With kinetic energy awaiting to be unshackled

He gently, tenderly cupped and caressed her face with his two
hands
As he passionately kissed her, but with a little reserve and
restraint

She had never felt so alive as she did at that exact singular
moment in time,
All of her synapses firing at hyper speed at the exact same
second

What felt like an eternity with being totally enveloped
In the moment came to a close much too soon for her

Softly, slowly, cordially the kiss ended
Gradually, hesitantly pulling his lips back from hers,
Her lips retained the faint lingering, residual imprint of his
lips against hers

Slowly opening her expressive, round radiantly emerald, green
eyes,
The flecks of burnished gold brightly gleaming,

She submissively gazed up at him and smiled

Her world would never be the same ever again
It has just been instantly, permanently,
Ultimately changed forever,

She had just experienced her very first kiss.

Her Magical Touch

Her fingertips caressed his very soul when they embraced.
Without saying a single word,
She would tell him her dreams with a kiss.

He would get lost in her touch.
He felt like he was home in her arms.
His senses would totally come to life when she was with him.

Her touch was a desire he never wanted to be without.
Her hands felt ethereally, magical when they would dance
across his skin.

Those were the moments that he truly felt alive.
It caused sensations he never wanted to end,
Passions flame burning bright inside.

Even after all these many years,
Their love remained undeniable for each other,
With wrinkles of age in her face and a full head of thick long
flowing silver, gray hair.
She was still that same strikingly, beautiful girl in his eyes, all
these years later.

He knew someday she would not be by his side.
Until that day, he couldn't live without her magical touch.

You Are My....

You are my shining light in the darkest times
The air my lungs breath
Blood coursing through my veins
Sun in the daylight
Moon in the sky at night
Shelter from the cold
Dry place when it rains

Hope for a better tomorrow
Reason to be a better person
Proof dreams come true
Answered prayer
Entire world
Unexpected gift
Best friend
Soulmate
Eternal love
That's what you are......

I Only Want to Dance with You

I want SLOW DANCING beneath the silvery moon,
You as my bride with me as your groom.
Let's BACHATA in the rain on a summer day.
SWING DANCE with me while life's music plays.

Be my TANGO partner for all eternity.
With you, there's no other place I ever want to be.
We'll FOXTROT in perfect rhythm dip and sway.
As years roll by, we'll CHA-CHA till our last day

In happy times, a fun JITTERBUG will do,
As your partner we can TWIST the night through.
Time constantly moves on it will never stop.
Your timing is perfect doing the LINDY HOP.

SALSA dancing with you as life plays its song.
Holding you close, as its music flows along.
Dancing close while its sexy rhythms play,
Our rhythms sync perfectly in PASO DOBLE.

MERENGUE with you touches deep in my heart.
Your dancing captured my soul from the start.
Through life, I only want to SAMBA with you.
Occasionally a sweet hot sexy MAMBO will do.

As WALTZ partners, we are the perfect pair,
To RUMBA daily with you has passions flair.
BOLERO steams from our souls clear through.
I want no other dance partner; I want only you.

The Ghost That Lives in My Soul

You're just a shadow of who I loved once upon a time
Long ago you would light up my entire world
Where did the passion go how did it disappear?

Now we live like spirits coexisting in the same house
you used to ignite a raging inferno of passion through my
heart
All that is there now is a frigid cold dark deep vacancy

What was my heart is now broken shards of metaphysical
pain,
Instead of passion filled looks of love
There are hate-filled stares of contempt and anger
Conversations containing laughter and love
Replaced with vitriol and vehemence or icy cold hours of
silence

Eyes that once sparkled shimmered with amorous delight
now burst with daggers of resentment disdain and hostility
A house that used to be a form of a warm paradise, feels like
a cold empty prison
The guardian of hope promise protection and security has
transformed
Into the ghost that lives in my soul.

A Fool for You

I am such a fool for you,
I'm lost and don't know what to do.

We've been friends for a long time,
It hurts that you will never be mine.

My heart wishes you would be with me,
Destiny's plan says it just wasn't to be.

You have chosen someone differently
Once again you overlooked me

All our lives we've known each other,
You've always thought of me like a brother.

You only want to just hold my hand,
To fall in love with me would just be grand.

When the special guy gets down on one knee,
And asks you the question, "Will you marry me?"

For you I will be so extremely happy,
I hope my tears you will not see.

Inside it will completely tear me apart,
I hope you don't hear my shattering heart.

A place inside my heart you'll always stay,
Until on this earth, I live my last day.

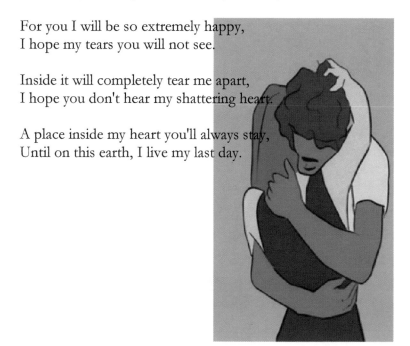

My Solid Rock

When my world is crumbling and falling apart
I feel lost and stranded alone in the dark
You are my anchor you're my salvation
You're my guiding light in my heart

I look to you and know you're my reason—
The one thing that makes me want to go on
Today's storm will try its best to break me
But, with you there's always sunlight at dawn

Confidence is gift that you freely give to me
Believing in me is simply what you always do
You have a way to leave me speechless
It's one of the reasons I am in love with you

Troubles and trials besiege me constantly
With you I face them you're my solid rock,
Like a ship tossed and lost out at sea
You're the light that guides me into the dock

Wrapped in your loving embrace I feel safe
Your arms are my sanctuary I can never replace
There is security and peaceful comfort,
When I look into your beautiful smiling face

You are my respite amidst the storms in life
A Zen like tranquility in all I've been through
A one-of-a-kind irreplaceable emotional haven
I hope these words say how much I love you

She Will Be Okay

Tears fell from her pain filled eyes
Like rain pouring down from a stormy sky
Hurt and pain are etched deep in her face
Her heart was broken and felt out of place

A cavernous hole was centered in her chest
Sleep would not come she just couldn't rest
Suddenly single no longer a future to be wife
Now she was in a quandary regarding her life

Time crawled slowly past as she lay in her bed
Confusion stormed frantically inside her head
He blindsided her saying that they were done
She would not sleep before the rising sun

Tossing and turning under the moonbeams
Grasping hopefully for nocturnal dreams
Racked with overwhelming emotional pain
Tonight, sleep will evade her time and again

In the morning she will rise and move on
It will be many days for this pain to be gone
Putting the past behind her each passing day
She's resilient a survivor she'll be perfectly okay

It Was Over

He left a final kiss on her forehead
She instantly realized it was a kiss goodbye
Time to part and go separate ways
Slowly been drifting far apart
Passion was gone smoldering ashes remain
Closing the door mirrored the end of them
Leaving his shattered heart outside her door

As the door clicked shut closing behind him
Torrents of tears streamed down her face
Dropping silently to her knees on the floor
Her body is racked with sobs continuously
She knew he was never returning it was over
Inside her chest her heart lay in broken pieces

Cold rain fell rhythmically pelting his face
Drenching his clothes tightly against his skin
Shambling shuffling down the street in the rain
Thoughts swirled searching for answers
Multitude of questions turbulently crashing
Soulmates from the moment they had met
What happened to the passion they shared?

As driving rain pounded against the windows
Her hands clenched tightly balled into fists
Throwing her head back emitting a scream
Grasping for answers that refused to come
She felt utterly lost and abandoned inside
Every individual fiber within her body ached
He had barely left, and she missed him already

Shoving his hands deep into his coat pockets
Shoulders hunched trudging down the street
Walking through puddles as the rain pelted him
He began to mourn their relationships end

Slowly unsteadily she arose from her knees
Resolutely she wiped salty tears from her face
She lamented it's finished,
Time to move on.

Forever Isn't Enough Time with You

I want to stay forever in this moment with you.
There's nothing else I really want to do.
Dancing under the millions of stars in the sky.
I get lost by pure unrequited love in your eyes.

With everything that we have been through,
I wish I could spend more than one lifetime with you.
My heart is on fire whenever you are near.
My love for you grows more every single year.

It still tingles like the first time when you said, "I love you."
I have been blessed since the day we said I do.
Not wanting to waste a moment of this life.
You're a heaven-sent angel I was given as my wife.

When I wrap my arms around you, I still get butterflies.
Their number is more than the stars in the sky.
When my life draws to a close, my days will be almost through.
My last words will be, "Forever isn't enough time with you."

Broken Pieces

When you left, it tore me up inside.
Never knew that a man could hurt so much.
I found out a person could cry so much—
Till no tears are left to fall.

Carnage you created was immense.
Pain I went through was monumental.
You will never comprehend its effect,
Or grasp the suffering I endured.

You destroyed my soul,
Shredded my beating heart—
Extinguishing all passion within.
Rendering my other emotions comatose.

My life fell into total disarray.
My entire world was in shambles.
It takes time for a person to heal.

It took all the strength I had within me
To forgive you.

Day-by-day, rebuilding who I am,
With the love lessons that I have learned.
I am stronger than I was,
Living with these broken pieces.

To Love Again

Love entered her world unexpectedly,
it caught her by surprise, completely breathlessly

So, she took a chance on love, it crushed and broke her heart
Shattered all her dreams, tore her world completely apart,

So in bed at night, she lays with the hurt and the pain,
Which is not being washed away by her tears that fall like rain

She doesn't know the reason he took his love and went away,
It was supposed to be for forever not to go but to stay

This world just keeps on turning and moving that is true,
Tomorrow she will begin again it's all that she can do.

You Said You'd Grow Old with Me

You left without saying a word,
it all happened so very suddenly
You never had a chance to say goodbye
The silence without you is deafening

You left me here alone by myself,
I am lost with no direction to go
You were the sunshine that lit up my world
Now there is only darkness every day

You left so many plans unfinished
They can't be completed by myself
You left so many dreams undone
So many memories we will never make

You took the best parts of me with you
There's a severe pain in me that never stops
You valiantly battled to the very end
I know you are finally at rest with no pain

You said you'd grow old with me
For now, I must travel life's road alone
Every passing hour and day does one thing
Brings me closer to the day I reunite with you

After All These Years

After all these years,
He didn't know when it did start.
His feelings for his best friend,
Had changed deep inside his heart

After all these years,
They had been best friends since childhood.
Had gone through everything together—
Some were bad, but most of it was good.

After all these years,
Together they went to their first high school dance.
They went simply as best friends.
There was no kissing and no romance.

After all these years,
Time seemed to fly for many years.
They shared many hours of laughter,
there were also times of many tears.

After all these years,
He watched as she dated many a guy.
All ended in total heartbreak,
On his shoulder, she would cry.

After all these years,
One night destiny gave him a shove.
He looked deeply, directly into her eyes—
Told her, "It's you that I truly love!"

After all these years,
She smiled, said, "I'm in love with you too;
I've loved you now for many years—
I don't want another day away from you.

After all these years,
They were more than friends.
Everyone could see they were perfectly matched soulmates,
Now together for the rest of eternity.

Momma Dance With Me

Momma dance with me
I will always be your son
My single days are over now
My married life has just begun

You've been in my life since I was born
You will remain first love of my life
But another woman now holds my heart
On this very day she has become my wife

Lessons that you taught me as I grew up
Showed me right from wrong at an early age
Have molded me into the man I have become
With another woman now I turn a new page

Momma dance with me
I will always be your son
My single days are over now
My married life has just begun
It's time for me to become a man
Pack all the toys of my childhood away
Where an innocent boy once stood
A young man dances with you today

From the first steps that I ever took
To the first words I was ever able to speak
You nurtured me all through these many years
Crafted me to be strong so I wouldn't be weak

Gave me confidence taught me about love
My guardian angel is who you will always be
You set the standard that I was searching for
Now I am with the woman meant for me

Momma dance with me
I will always be your son
My single days are over now
My married life has just begun
You taught me one day I would find
Someone to be with rest of my life through
Momma the wait sure worth all the pain
Because she reminds me so much of you

She will be my new forever dance partner
From this day forward til death do us part
But I will always save a dance for you
On the dance card I keep in my heart

Hope you're proud of the man here before you
No one will ever take your place with me
Momma please don't cry to many tears
I will dance with you anytime for all eternity

Momma dance with me
I will always be your son
My single days are over now
My married life has just begun
This dance with you is not our last
There will be many more in the years to come
I want you to always remember one thing
I'm may be married now, but I will always be your son

Til We Meet Again

He sat as his mind raced back over the years
His eyes welled up with untold sad tears
Thinking of memories from times gone by
A melancholy expression with a heavy sigh

Faces of friends one by one flickered past,
He never anticipated that he would be last
Places he had been things they had done
Came back as he watched the setting sun

Where had the time gone; he had grown old
He lived a magical life from the stories he told
Traveled around the globe and raised a family
Tales of his adventures would make a movie

The moon rose and stars filled the night sky
Down his cheek rolled a tear from his eye
Another day was ending almost time for bed
He would dream of his friends inside his head

One of these days from this world he'll depart
Reunited with his friends with joy in his heart
Reminiscing with stories and feeling their love
It'll be a magnificent day up there high above

A Summer Night (Moments With You)

Summer breeze wafting around
Fireflies flickering dancing
Stars twinkling in the night sky
Barefoot on emerald green grass

Whisper of a kiss
Taste of your tongue
Brush of your crimson lips
Breath dancing on my cheek

Your head against my chest
My chin resting atop of your head
Nestled in your auburn tresses
Inhaling your hairs jasmine fragrance

Our fingers interlocked
Bodies pressed tightly together
Swaying gently in unison
In perfect rhythm with the night

Moonlights pale glow
Illuminating your beautiful face
Sapphire eyes shining brightly
Starlight reflected within them

Treasuring this second
Time frozen in its tracks
Hands on the clock stopped
Mentally taking a photograph

Saving this for posterity
Image I will never forget
Permanently ensconced
In my cranium forever

Special encapsulated snippets
Priceless invaluable memories
Private moments with you
Snapshots like this I live for

On a summer night

Return To Love

I lived within a world of doubt
No longer did I truly believe
That light would ever shine in my life
Then came the day you appeared
You were the spark that reignited my flame

I was reluctant to willingly take the risk
Not wanting my heart again to break
I decided to take a monumental leap of faith
For a reward that I thought was unattainable
My heart opened and returned to love

Flames within grew into a roaring inferno
You resuscitated feelings and emotions
Reinvigorating desires that were dormant
Passion was rekindled inside my soul
Existence was given a seminal purpose

I'm willing to take this chance and maybe fall
Trusting that my heart you will not break
To see a world the two of us can make
Take my hand in yours from this moment on
There are many memories for us yet to make

Even though I am still scared and afraid
With you I find the courage to face it all
Precious moments with you I treasure
Let's make this love last for all eternity
With you I have a reason to return to love.

My Love's Kisses

Addicting
Constantly
Craving
Never Enough
Emotionally

        Passions
        Inferno
        Ignited
        Delicately
        Rose petal texture

Silky soft
Kittens fur
Syrupy sweet
Unrefined honey
Comfortingly warm
Summer sunshine

        Full Body flavor
        Tastefully
        Reminiscent
        Fine wine

Fragile
Angels touch
Toes curled up
Finger tips tingling
Electrifying

        Light headed
        Tranquil sensations
        Physically relaxing

Effervescent
Waterfall cooling
Serene ambiance
In my soul

Searing heat
Devil's fire
Heart warming
Sip of cognac
Expanding gradually
In my chest

Passion's Flame

The passion of love burned bright deep inside her
It was an ache that radiated outward
from her very soul, throughout her entire body
An all-consuming constantly burning desire to be loved

She wanted someone would return that love to her
A strong pair of arms to embrace her and wrap around her
tightly
Arms that she could get lost in, to wash away the day
To lay her head against his chest
Listening to the rhythmic beating of his heart

She ached to kissed with the fire of passions
Intense unquenchable heat and desire
The type of kiss you wish, dream pray and fantasize about
A kiss to awaken her raw, carnal, primal desires and emotions
buried deep in her soul
Yearning to be released from their prison and set free

She thirsts to be physically and emotionally swept off her feet
To be completely enveloped and transported
to that mystical realm of unbridled unrelenting passion

Her longing for this had gone unquenched her entire life
With each passing year, she remained unattached
She had started to resolutely accept that it was not to be
In her bed each night she would lay there alone and dream

Slowly, unhurriedly, unbidden bitter tears
Filled with heartache regret and anguish would
Escape the corners of her eyes and gradually,
Trickle sliding down the sides of her face,
Gently falling onto her pillow
This has become her nightly ritual, a tear
Stained pillow was her reward as she drifted off to sleep

Every single morning, she would awake with hope and a
silent prayer
Hopefully that today would be her day finally
Telling herself this was the day her man of mystery and
destiny would appear.
That passions bright flame that burned inside her,
Would finally summon him to her.

Missing You

Your memories still run through my veins
Your spirit still lives in my heart
There's a raw emptiness in my soul,
Now that we are apart

Days used to be happy and bright
Now they're just all sad and gray
I wonder why I am still here,
Since you have been taken away

The fight we had that morning I regret
I was wrong to have caused so much pain
I wish you would have stayed with me,
Instead of driving off in the pouring rain

I called your cell phone but you never answered
Just wanted a chance to talk and explain
It was later when I learned of the accident
You crashed with the oncoming train

My heart broke into a million pieces
I cried so hard that I could not see
Dropped to my knees in total disbelief,
There was no longer an us, now , there was only me

My heart, soul and world were shattered
Never again kiss your lips, your voice I'll never hear
You're physically gone from this world
I can feel your spirit's still here

What used to be a warm and happy house
No longer has energy, it's lifeless and cold
We were supposed to be for forever
Our dream was together we would grow old

Some days that I can smile
Days that I cry a tear or two
I hope from this pain, one day I will heal
Until then I will live life missing you

Grow Old with You

Take my hand, take my heart.
From you, I never want to be apart.
If I was a bird with two broken wings,
I would find a way to you through anything.

You're my beacon, a bright shining light—
My lamp of goodness in my darkest night.
There isn't a fire that I wouldn't walk through,
As long as I know I could get to you.

As long as my lungs can draw a breath,
I'll love you forever even beyond death.
Longer than celestial stars twinkle above,
For eternity plus one second, it's you I love.

I am amazed at just how lucky I did get,
When we locked eyes the first night we met.
God in his plans, joined together us two.
I'm blessed in my life to grow old with you

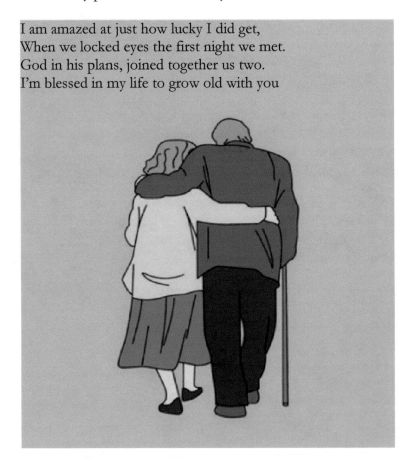

I'm Always Here

Physically from this world I am gone,
but spiritually I'm still very much here.
When you think of me, I hope you smile,
I don't want you to shed a single tear.

In winter, I'm the frost on your windows.
Also, the glistening white snow on Christmas Day,
With spring budding trees and beautiful flowers,
Singing birds and squirrels happily at play.

Summer, I'm the hot sun that browns your skin.
Long lazy pool days, fun filled nights
In autumn, I'm colorful leaves falling from trees,
Hanging out with friends by the bonfire lights.

When you're deep asleep in bed at night,
I protect and keep you safe in your dream.
You only need to softly whisper my name,
I'm your personal guardian angel supreme.

No matter what happens wherever you are,
You'll never be alone nor have anything to fear.
Physically, I may no longer be by your side.
Spiritually, I will always be with you right here.

Til The End of Time

I feel a spiritual connection with you.
When I gaze deep into your pain-filled eyes.
Let me see the shadows inside your heart,
To see the real you, underneath your disguise.

Lay all your emotions open and naked.
Reveal all the secrets hidden in your soul.
Let me pour my love into your darkness,
Heal the tortured pain that's taken a huge toll.

Trust that I will love you like no other.
In time, passion's flame in you, I will reignite.
Soft kisses and caresses are only the start.
It will happen slowly—over many a day and night.

You tell me that you're broken and damaged—
Not to waste my time and energy on you.
In your ear, I whisper my response quietly,
"I am going to present you a love you've never felt or knew."

Take you to amorous levels of passion you never realized
existed.
Releasing desires, you were afraid to reveal,
Emotions that had been deeply locked away,
that I need you to grasp deal with and feel.

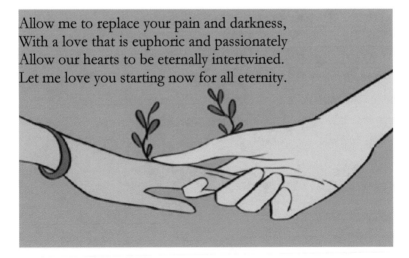

Allow me to replace your pain and darkness,
With a love that is euphoric and passionately
Allow our hearts to be eternally intertwined.
Let me love you starting now for all eternity.